WITH A
Dog's
Love

Clever
Dogs Helping
Humans

First published in 2021 by New Holland Publishers

Sydney • Auckland

Level 1, 178 Fox Valley Road, Wahroonga 2076, Australia
5/39 Woodside Ave, Northcote, Auckland 0627, New Zealand

newhollandpublishers.com

A record of this book is held at the National Library of Australia.

ISBN 9781760793654

Group Managing Director: Fiona Schultz
Publisher: Arlene Gippert
Designer: Yolanda la Gorcé
Project Editor: Liz Hardy
Production Director: Arlene Gippert

Printed in China

10 9 8 7 6 5 4 3 2 1

Keep up with New Holland Publishers:

 NewHollandPublishers

@newhollandpublishers

New Holland Publishers are extremely proud supporters of the Starlight Children's Foundation and the purchase of this book generates proceeds to further help Starlight, *"Brighten the lives of seriously ill children and their families."*
starlight.org.au

WITH A
Dog's
Love

Clever
Dogs Helping
Humans

GINA DAWSON

DEDICATED TO FRIENDSHIP

With love and appreciation to a
handful of incredibly special friends.
You know who you are.

ACKNOWLEDGEMENTS

Many thanks to RICHARD TAPP for undertaking
what turned into the enormous task of
photo editing for this book.
Images page 1, page 76 and cover: Kiera,
the author's assistance dog.
Photographs by Richard Tapp.

INTRODUCTION

Every dog that is loved and cared for makes a difference to our lives. Dogs want to be with us and to please us. They make good mates. They make us laugh. They keep us healthy by getting us outdoors to walk or play with them. They supply endless cuddles. Their love is unconditional, and they never judge us. They ask for little in return: kindness, a comfy bed, exercise, and regular meals. And love.

With a dog at your side, you have an amazing friend.

But some dogs do a little bit more. They aren't always dogs who make the front-page news with heroics. Instead, they quietly go about their lives, willingly doing their best to help humans in a way they have been trained to do and want to do. As the saying goes, 'we do for them and they do for us'. A perfect partnership.

From dogs that help one person to lead a life that may not have been possible, through to dogs that touch the lives of many, the dogs in this book are the quiet heroes.

I hope you enjoy the stories of these incredibly special dogs.

Gina Dawson

Assistance dog Bruno.

CONTRIBUTORS

A huge thank you to the below contributors, without whom this book would not have been possible.

(Listed in order of appearance in this book)

ALEX SCHANZER NZUSAR	(Bryn)
ADAM JAY COURT	(Jacob)
LORIS PHAIR	(Hermione)
CHRIS BLACKHAM-DAVISON	(Tamari)
EMMA BROE	(Bruno)
JODI McDONALD	(Flash)
CATH FLANAGAN	(Baz)
KHASHIA FORSYTH – aged 12	(Moby)
CAROLINE KIEFER	(Kelsi)
CATH PHILLIPS	(Buddy)
PETA BAXTER	(Frank)
JAMES RIACH	(Max)
LYNNE WILLIAMS	(Alice)
DONNA HOWARD	(Ebony)
ELIZABETH SMITH	(Gidget)
CHARLIE SERRAVITE	(Hunter)

CONTENTS

8

27

23

14

BRYN — WITH A BIT OF LOVE AND CARE ANYTHING IS POSSIBLE

On a drizzly day, a tiny, bedraggled puppy, only days old, weaved between traffic on a busy street. A woman saw him, darted out and scooped him to safety, doubtless saving his life. She took him to the shelter, where the starving and sickly pup needed round-the-clock care. He was shared between foster homes until, three months later, he was pronounced healthy and ready to find his forever home.

I'm Alex, a K9 handler and trainer for New Zealand Urban Search and Rescue. I was at the shelter, looking for a dog with a difference. My future dog needed to have loads of energy, be motivated and smart, love solving problems for reward and be pretty much fearless – all the things that cause dogs to get into heaps of trouble!

I hadn't found a dog that day and was leaving when I noticed the puppy section. A lanky pup approached the window, tail wagging and alert eyes watching me closely. There was something about him that made me stop and ask if I could meet him. I was sitting, waiting, when the gate opened and the pup bolted through at full speed, raced around the enclosure, nose down and investigating. Satisfied, he stopped, turned towards me and stared. From a standing start he was off again, galloping towards me and launching himself onto my lap! Thwack! How could I leave that dog behind?

When Bryn came home it didn't take long to see that he was determined, intense, smart, learned fast, wanted to be in the thick of everything and had way too much energy. If Bryn wasn't occupied in doing something to use his brain and energy, he would be getting up to mischief. Bryn needed a challenging job!

I remembered when the city was rocked by earthquake some years earlier. Buildings collapsed and people were injured and killed. People from around the world had come to help search for survivors, trapped under collapsed buildings and rubble. With them were search dogs. This was a job that Bryn could learn to do, and perhaps an opportunity to help others.

Bryn grew up to be better at his job than anyone could ever have imagined. Bryn's job title is Live Find Specialist. His job is to find trapped people who have survived natural disasters, such as earthquakes, landslides, avalanches or floods. It's a job that takes years of training, regular practice and loads of fitness, skill and enthusiasm.

Bryn and I joined the training program when Bryn was nine months old. He passed all tests with flying colours and began 18 months of intense training, including obedience, agility, rubble awareness, working in difficult situations and learning to search for live human scent. His light paws and size mean he can get into places that people cannot. He learned to climb up and down ladders, crawl through dark tunnels and cramped areas, be lowered down holes, hoisted in harness into buildings, to abseil with me down structures, ride in helicopters and search planes, and work in extreme conditions.

The weird thing is that after all that training, everyone hopes Bryn will never have to do his job for real! If he does, it means that there has been a natural disaster, and no-one wants that to happen.

Bryn and I need total trust in each other when we undertake these dangerous tasks. I need to know that Bryn will do anything and go anywhere I send him to search, and he must trust me completely and follow orders, however scary they may seem. That's what makes him an exceptional dog. It's a huge ask!

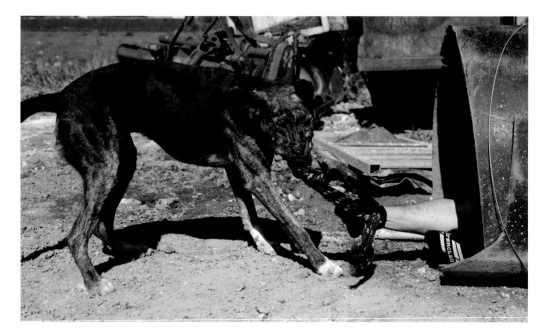

Bryn doesn't wear a jacket or collar when he works as they could get caught on something and trap him. When he detects live human scent, he barks so the human search party know where to look and keeps on barking until help arrives. Sometimes he helps by digging or dragging people from tricky situations.

After four years Bryn is one of only seven dogs to have reached this specialist level in New Zealand. He could be deployed here or overseas as part of Task Force 1. Nature will decide if he ever sees active service, but we are ready if needed to do our bit.

When Bryn isn't working, he's a happy, healthy dog that loves cuddles, running on the beach, snoozing, and playing chase with his doggy mate Tama.

From an unwanted pup, dumped and left to die, Bryn has emerged a skilled and fearless dog who, if disaster strikes, will be on the front line, helping save lives. It just goes to show that with a bit of love and care, anything is possible.

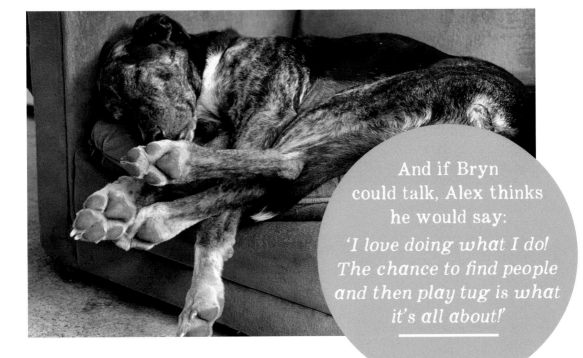

And if Bryn could talk, Alex thinks he would say:

'I love doing what I do! The chance to find people and then play tug is what it's all about!'

2

JACOB — OUR LITTLE MIRACLE

Miracles come in all shapes and sizes. There are big miracles, like surviving a plane crash and being found wandering in the bush two weeks later. Now that would be a big miracle. But then there are small miracles. Four-legged, soft, golden, furry, wet-nosed, warm-eyed type of miracles. That's Jacob, our Labrador. He's our family's small miracle.

I'm Adam, the dad of Isaac and Isla. Jacob came to live with us three years ago when Isaac was six and Isla was four. Isaac and Isla have autism spectrum disorder. That means they see the world differently to most of us. Sometimes that's a good thing, because they see and understand things that we don't, but often it can make the world seem like a confusing and scary place.

That's why we have Jacob. When things get scary, it's natural to want comfort from someone we trust, and for Isaac and Isla that someone is their best friend, Jacob.

Jacob is an autism assistance dog. He goes everywhere with our family: to the shops, on the train, the public swimming pool – people get dressed quickly when a big dog enters the change room! – on aeroplanes with the human passengers, stays in motel rooms and goes to fancy restaurants too!

Jacob had a lot of training before he came to live with us. He knows he needs to be calm and patient wherever he goes. Jacob will lay quietly under the table at a restaurant for two hours without begging or drooling for the food being served above him.

Busy places with lots of noises, movements and smells can be overwhelming for people on the autism spectrum, and restaurants have all those things. Early on, Isaac would sometimes get under the

table with Jacob. He would rest his head on Jacob's chest and listen to his heartbeat, his head moving up and down with the gentle rise and fall of Jacob's chest.

Usually, people don't know there is a dog amongst them until we get up to leave. That's how quiet and still Jacob can be. He knows how to blend in and not draw attention to himself as he goes about helping us with day-to-day activities.

Jacob was chosen because he is intelligent, responsible, calm and loving, characteristics needed by autism assistance dogs. When his training was complete, Isaac and Isla spent two weeks with Jacob and his trainers, so everyone could get to know each other and give Jacob the very best chance of helping our family. We parents needed to learn as well, as we are responsible for Jacob when he is out in public.

Twice each year we receive a visit from someone from Righteous Pups to see how Jacob is going. That's so he can keep his assistance dog licence up to date. He needs that licence so he can go everywhere that we go.

One time our family was sightseeing and Jacob was beside me. A tourist tiptoed up to me, crouched down and took a selfie of herself with Jacob and me. She thought I was blind and could not see her. Another time I arrived at a hotel with Jacob and the receptionist linked arms with me, ready to guide me to my room. Some people think that assistance dogs are only for people who can't see!

Although both Isaac and Isla are autistic, they have quite different personalities. It's amazing to watch Jacob behaving differently with each of them. If Isaac is upset Jacob cheers him up by jumping and spinning in circles. Isaac loves to watch that. Isaac now has the confidence to talk to other people in the park who have dogs, so his communication skills have improved heaps.

Isla likes to chill out and draw in her room, so Jacob can often be found lying beside her, wrapped in a quilted blanket, wearing a princess tiara on his head.

Thanks to Jacob, Isaac and Isla sleep in their own beds at night. If they get scared, they can reach out their hand and their furry buddy Jacob will be there for a cuddle until they drift back to sleep. Eating out and sleeping at night are things most families take for granted, but for our family each time it happens it is like a little miracle. That's because we remember when even these things felt impossible and overwhelming!

And if Jacob could speak, Isaac (9) and Isla (7) think he would say: *'I love my family. I love taking care of you and being your assistance dog. Thank you for taking good care of me!'*

For Isaac and Isla, having a companion who is always there, never judges them and seems to understand them even when others don't – well, that's the miracle of friendship.

FRANK — THE FRISKY, FREE-THINKING FRUG

F rank always had a strong will and ideas of his own. His first human family declared him a handful, a naughty dog looking for mischief, causing damage, refusing to learn his lessons and out of control. Frank, a cross between a French bulldog and a pug, had to go. Figuring that he couldn't be as bad as all that, my partner adopted him.

Obedience school was a flop. Frank was kicked out of class for misbehaving and pronounced untrainable. Private lessons failed. Frank refused to cooperate and learned nothing.

At home Frank caused havoc. He constantly escaped, sneaking between legs and darting through doors. Running down the street as fast as his legs would take him, he ignored the frantic calls of people chasing him. He jumped on visitors, chewed everything, and if he was feeling lazy or cold, peed in all the wrong places. Despite these problems, we loved Frank and wouldn't part with him, so we lurched from crisis to crisis.

I'm Peta, and I'm a kindergarten teacher. A photo of Frank on my laptop screensaver began this story. The children loved Frank's photo and constantly asked if Frank could visit kindy. I wasn't keen. Keeping track of disobedient Frank alongside 22 children – well, let's say much could go wrong. But the children pleaded. Frank is a gentle dog who wouldn't hurt anyone, so we arranged for him to visit kindy as my special show and tell.

Every work morning, Frank put on a doleful face as I edged my way out the front door, so he was super excited when he realised that he was coming with me that day. At kindy he raced about, nose down, ignoring us as usual, and checking out the smells in the playground and inside.

Children began arriving, excited to meet Frank, and an astounding thing happened! Frank didn't jump on people or misbehave. He didn't try to sneak through the gate, chew the kindy toys or pee on anything! This was a side of Frank he'd never shown: Frank behaving perfectly. The children instantly fell in love with him.

There were no tearful children holding onto parents that day. In fact, children were cheerfully telling parents to leave so they could play with Frank.

Then, a second surprise. At group time Frank chose to sit on the mat with the children. He watched me as I read books and listened to us singing songs, just like he was part of the class. During inside play, Frank was inside. During outside play he went out. At rest time, he chose a bed and snuggled in for a nap. Every moment brought new surprises. Some children feared dogs and Frank stayed away, happily being with children who wanted him nearby.

That afternoon the children said goodbye to Frank, and he watched them leave without a fuss. Perfect Frank. The next morning the children spoke of nothing but Frank and implored me to bring him again. The decider was seeing children who had cheerfully waved their parents off the day before, holding onto their parents and crying again.

So, Frank became a kindy dog. The words 'It's a kindy day Frank' are enough to have him bouncing on the spot with enthusiasm and impatience to get going.

At kindy Frank is cheeky and playful, but also relaxed. He offers comfort and cuddles to children who are upset. Instead of distracting the children, Frank keeps them focused. He sits with children who have trouble sitting still, and they relax and listen as they pat him.

Frank loves to join in. He loves children's tea parties, getting his hair done in their pretend salon and listening to reading. He has learned many words. Children build block houses around him. They draw around him with chalk on the concrete. He poses to be drawn and painted. There are plasticine Franks, cards made featuring Frank, and beaded necklaces made for Frank. And of course, Frank must be part of the kindergarten class photo!

The children say Frank is the best thing about kindy. Thanks Frank! They are responsible for his water bowl, food and regular baths. They have learned to be gentle with animals, understand their feelings and much more.

Three years on we can't imagine kindy without Frank. He brings smiles and laughter to faces every day. When the kindy doorbell rings, Frank races to greet visitors and put a smile on their face.

And it goes both ways. Kindy is Frank's special place where he receives love and attention and uses his mischievous energy. Frank found his place and his purpose as a kindy dog. Now five years old, his free-thinking, friendly manner makes a difference as he gets things done – his way.

At home, Frank no longer runs away or behaves naughtily. He has transformed from a Frug who flopped to a perfectly mannered dog! And he did it all by himself!

And if Frank could talk, Peta thinks he would probably say:

'Is it kindy day? Hurry up, hurry up! Get me dressed and let's get going. The children are waiting for me! What's the hold-up? Yay yay it's kindy day!'

And straight from the dog's mouth ...

TAMARI — RAGS TO RICHES AND PROUD OF IT

I'm Tamari, a heeler Staffordshire cross. Nobody knows exactly when or where I was born, because I was unwanted, uncared for and abandoned. Next thing, I was looking through the bars of a cage in an animal shelter, feeling very afraid.

But one day I got lucky. A veterinarian who was at the shelter noticed me. He soon figured I was a smart, intelligent dog with a nice nature, and decided to give me a chance at life. He took me home and organised for me to go to a special dog school, to see if I had what it takes to be a hearing assistance dog, a dog that helps someone who is deaf.

I was happy to be safe and looked after and excited to be going to school. I practised my obedience lessons and soon moved on to learning all the new skills needed for me to become a hearing dog. I learnt to recognise sounds such as doorbells, telephones, ovens, alarm clocks and lots of others.

Some days I went on outings, wearing my official Lions Hearing Dog coat, to practise behaving in public places. I visited shopping centres, rode on lifts, climbed stairs, and waited quietly at checkouts. I ignored people and focused on my trainer. I went to restaurants and learned not to beg or drool. That was a tricky one, as the wonderful smells made my nose twitch!

And after lots and lots of learning, finally I was ready to start life helping a deaf person! How proud I was to hear people say what an obedient and clever dog I was.

The man I would help lived 3000 kilometres away in a world of silence. He could not hear a sound. He slept through storms and even a cyclone. He was born deaf and has never heard sound. He used lipreading and sign language to communicate. He lived alone and didn't hear when his doorbell or telephone rang, the microwave pinged, or the smoke alarm went off. He decided that a hearing dog would make his life easier and safer, and he wouldn't miss all those sounds.

I travelled with my trainer by aeroplane, on the floor of the cabin next to him. I was the only dog in the cabin and felt lucky because other dogs travelled in the hold with the freight. Being in an aeroplane for the first time was a little bit scary, but my trainer was calm, so I stayed calm too.

When we landed, we headed off by car to meet Chris, the deaf human I was going to help. We were soon at his house, and the moment I saw him I fell instantly in love with him. I was so excited to see him that I forgot all my manners and how to do my job! I thought I was on a holiday! But when I calmed down, I slowly came to understand that this was to be my new forever home.

The three of us spent a week together. I learned where things were around my new house and the sounds that they made. Then I practised identifying the sounds. When I heard a sound, I responded by running to Chris, tapping or jumping on him, and leading him to the sounds. I loved alerting Chris to sounds because when I did my job well it made him happy, plus I'd receive a treat. Yum! Bring on more sounds!

That first week we all went on outings too, so I could get to know the local area. It was fun meeting new people! I rode on the bus and visited the shopping centres, restaurants and even the hospital.

That was all seven years ago, and what a wonderful seven years they have been. Chris and I still go everywhere together, including to Chris's work at the nearby school. I have even flown to other countries! I've seen a lion in South Africa – that was scary! I've seen the mud pools of New Zealand. I love adventures and will go anywhere, so long as I can be with Chris.

I'm proud that I've come from being an abandoned dog to one who is doing an important job. Now Chris relies on me and doesn't need people to tell him about important sounds. But better than that, we are best mates, and our days are full of love and cuddles.

And one last thing. Remember the veterinarian who rescued me? I heard that he has rescued 5000 cats and dogs from shelters and saved their lives. That's amazing too! I reckon he's a hero!

Me? I was given the chance to work and learn, and since then life has been a dog's version of a rags to riches story. It's a story that I'm proud to share with you.

5

BRUNO — PLAYING THE FOOL TO MAKE THINGS RIGHT

I live in a rain forest, in a secret house that no-one knows. I don't cope well with noise, public places or crowds of people. Here in the forest, it's peaceful.

I'm Emma. As a six-year-old, I overheard my teacher whisper that I was a very strange child, with odd ideas. Since then, I've experienced many traumas that are hard to forget. Mix it all together, and sure, I'm a little different. But that's okay! We don't all have to be the same, do we?

Bruno entered my life three years ago. I wanted a dog to help me on my road to recovery. But Bruno caused havoc from the start. After a week he vanished. I searched frantically before noticing the fridge door was partly open. I looked in. Bruno had climbed in to search for treats and fallen asleep on the bottom shelf.

He was a roly-poly bundle of fur who was always acting the fool. He would do the craziest things, like running indoors backwards with his bowl in his mouth, flipping it on his nose and departing the same way – backwards. I would watch in silent amazement. His imagination was endless. In he'd come, carrying his full water bowl without spilling a drop, then tipping it on my feet.

Training did not go well. He refused to take it seriously, his pranks becoming more and more outlandish. I employed a trainer, who said he would never be the dog I wanted him to be. I then contacted Whiskey's Wish, an organisation that helps people who have had trauma to train a dog as an assistance dog. It was there that I learned what Bruno was up to when he played the fool. He could sense my sadness and was trying to make me laugh. As soon as I laughed the antics stopped and he wagged his tail. Job done. He'd made me happy.

From that breakthrough we went ahead and together passed the Public Access Test. Now Bruno could come with me wherever I went. The clown act stops as soon as I put on his vest. Bruno takes control, looking up at me and encouraging me. If I hesitate to enter a building, he gently pulls me forward. Now I go to shopping centres. Bruno acts as my boundary and always puts himself in front if people get too close.

Every morning Bruno comes for cuddles. He sits with me all night if I can't sleep and is beside me when I'm restless and decide on a midnight walk. He calms me if I have flashbacks by putting his weight on my legs to let me know he's there, licks my tears, wakes me from nightmares and continues to play the fool to make me laugh.

Bruno helps me daily. I've had a broken back, and Bruno has learned to stand still so I can use him as a support to help me get up. He walks one step at a time as we attempt the stairs, and when I overdo our walks, pulls me along our track so I can make it home.

I was a volunteer for the State Emergency Service for seven years, helping people after floods, cyclones or other disasters. Towards the end of that time, Bruno attended a week-long public display and celebration with me, wearing his vest. It was the first time I had attended, being unable to cope with crowds before that, and with Bruno at my side I was able to demonstrate to the public the work that the SES does.

Meeting Bruno has been the start of my new life. I go to work each day and get things done. I speak out about mental health and encourage others to do so. I pushed for mental health first aid to become part of SES first-aid training, and after two years this happened.

But hey, it's not all serious – how could it be with Bruno playing the fool whenever he can? On rainy days he likes to do a little painting, dancing on sheets with paint on his feet. He loves watching me make papier-mâché, but then wants to eat it. He wanted to help with pottery but bit a chunk out of the clay of his newly formed dinner bowl as it dried. He loves our trips in the ute, cruising, tongue out lolling. He's brave and devoted and always looks out for me. And is the same dog who needs his paw held during thunderstorms and his 'bunny' with him as he sleeps.

I love living in a rainforest, surrounded by nature and with Bruno as my friend. I cannot imagine a more beautiful way to live.

And if Bruno could talk, Emma thinks he would say: *'Look, look at me! (tail wag) It's good to see you laugh!'*

FLASH — ACCEPTANCE IS A POWERFUL THING

Flash is a dog with many jobs. He attends school, but he isn't a school dog. I'm Jodi, a teacher, and Flash is my assistance dog.

Before Flash, my students were used to having relief teachers. They made so many get-well cards they were known as The Card Class. I was often in hospital. I would sleep for days, exhausted. I spent time and money on specialists yet still couldn't do everyday things like grocery shopping without help.

Then came Flash. Now I am at school every day. Flash is a huge help to me, but he cannot cure my disease. Life for me includes pain, difficulty with movement, severe spasms in my leg and more. Flash is a medical alert, mobility and mental health dog rolled into one.

If I'm alone and need help, Flash dashes to the school office to alert someone. If it's not safe to leave me, he knocks the handset off the landline phone, dials the office with his paw and barks when they answer. Flash is my security guard, who keeps me safe. Knowing help is near has changed my life. Now I can do my job and be self-sufficient. That feels wonderful!

It was my doctor who suggested an assistance dog might help with tasks I couldn't do. With encouragement from family and my school principal, I decided to try. Waiting lists for trained dogs were long, so I decided to train my own dog, and arranged an expert trainer to help me do this.

Next, I needed a dog. I let people know of my plans, and a breeder with a four-week-old litter of puppies contacted me. Off we went to

meet the pups. One black pup plonked his bottom on my foot, then followed at my heels. I knew this was the pup for me. Sadly, he was already promised to a family, and we left feeling a little dejected.

That evening the phone rang. It was the breeder, telling me the pup was mine. The family had heard my story and wanted me to have him. We were watching a show called *The Flash* on television when the call came, so we named our new hero-to-be Flash.

A month later, Flash was home. He was happy-go-lucky, smart, and learned quickly, especially when there was food involved! Flash loves food! He also loves attention and being busy. And so, training began.

My spasms occur without warning, and almost always mean a hospital stay. Flash's powerful nose can smell a chemical change in my body about an hour beforehand. Then he brings me my medication bag and I know what to do to prevent the spasm. Flash's nose has saved many a day.

At home, Flash lays along my leg and applies pressure, which eases pain. He tells me it's medication time, opening the fridge and fetching my water bottle. He brings icepacks from the freezer when I ask. He picks things up from the floor, finds my keys, phone and purse, turns lights on and off, and opens doors and cupboards. He's learning to load and unload the washing machine.

Flash came into my life when I needed him most, yet it feels like we've always known each other. He's my best friend, who knows all my secrets and would never tell!

Flash spends most of the school day on his bed, watching me. My students are incredibly respectful and supportive of Flash, and never distract him while he wears his vest. Even at school, Flash has work breaks. The vest comes off and he is free to wander and join in the fun. When he joined in a game of Bullrush, the squeals of laughter as he dodged, weaved and tripped students brought people from all around. Flash single-handedly won the game, which was recounted as a favourite memory at graduation that year.

Flash loves bananas. It's amazing how often a piece accidentally falls from a desk as he wanders by. He looks to me for permission to eat it. Except once! Flash spied a whole banana. I was too slow to respond, and it was too much to resist. He stepped on one end and slipped it out of its peel, and down it went in two lip-licking gulps. Naughty Flash!

Flash brightens our classroom and has brought about a strong sense of community at school. He tackles all tasks with enthusiasm, lives to please everyone and doesn't discriminate against anyone. He inspires students with special needs or disabilities, as they see first-hand that they also can become teachers, or anything they want to be. 'Acceptance is a powerful thing.' (*The Flash*)

With Flash I have many plans, but right now am happy being a teacher with Flash, my amazing sidekick, the hero who makes it all possible.

And if **Flash** could speak, Jodi thinks he would say: *'I'm doing what I love doing most for the person I love. What life could be better than that? Now, is there a banana anywhere?'*

7

BAZ — WORKING HIS MAGIC ON THE END OF A LEAD

Baz loves the park. He also loves playing ball. The park means Baz can find unsuspecting victims to throw the ball for him. His favourite ball throwers are kids. They are less likely to end the game and never tell him it's time to go home. Watching Baz at the park one day, I figured he could use up his endless energy by having a job.

I'm Cath, and I think of myself as Baz's personal assistant. Baz is outgoing, eager to please and loves people. Pet therapy, which is all about cuddles, snuggles and helping a sick person feel better, seemed like a good fit. That was if Baz could pass the interview and assessment. He can be naughty and a little bit bossy at times. Being naughty or bossy is not the best feature for a therapy dog. But Baz took it all in his stride. He coped with noisy trolleys and trundling wheelchairs and the unfamiliar smells around an aged-care home.

Together we were endorsed by Lort Smith Pet Therapy. The next step was the real deal, our first visit to a children's hospital. We almost didn't get past the front door. We approached the hospital, ready to meet the challenge. Baz had other ideas.

The rotating door was a showstopper. Baz stopped and refused to budge. Minutes later we entered the hospital, me carrying an 18 kg wriggling fluff-ball! Not a professional start! Paws back on the floor, things improved. Baz handled the greeting of office staff with ease.

Next challenge was the lift. Baz wasn't sure about this contraption, so we watched the doors open and close as people came and went. Okay, time we give this a try.

The doors opened and we strode purposefully to the lift. Baz stopped short. I imagined a repeat of the revolving door. Then Baz spied a chip on the lift floor. Whoever had dropped it saved the day. Baz bustled in. Since that day Baz marches into lifts, hopeful of reliving that chip experience.

We spent a wonderful year visiting that hospital. Baz stayed close and comforted children as they had treatments, stitches, or plaster on broken limbs. Many sick children smiled when they saw Baz.

There was the teenage boy, sedated and very unwell after a car accident. His mother and aunt sat watching him. I put Baz onto the bed. He snuggled in beside the boy, tucking his nose under his elbow. His mother talked to her unconscious son about the lovely fluffy dog. A few moments later, the nurse said, 'Well, look at that, his blood pressure is coming down.' I watched in awe, and behind me heard tears of happiness.

Baz won the heart of a six-year-old girl, who had a nasty virus and needed a machine to help her breathe. Baz visited weekly, laying close, and she rubbed him with her feet. Each week we saw improvement and the family enjoyed Baz's visits too, watching the calming effect Baz had on the girl.

There was laughter too. A girl, needing to build strength in her arms, was in a session that involved her picking up and throwing a ball. This was hard work and boring for her. Enter Baz. It was way more exciting to throw the ball for Baz, and for him to bring it back to her. The hospital room was full of giggles and fun as the session became a game, with Baz enjoying a ballgame with an eager ball-throwing child.

Baz attended art therapy and a girl drew many pictures of him. Such was her love for Baz, her parents decided to get a spoodle when she went home.

After a year, we began visiting another hospital. Baz quickly learned which staff members kept a stash of treats for him and made a point of greeting them when he arrived.

Here Baz met a lady, who was far from home for her treatment. She missed her own dog terribly, so Baz tried to fill the gap. It worked. Every week, the lady waited for Baz before attending her treatment session. When she was well, she returned to the hospital for a final visit and four years later Baz still receives birthday and Christmas cards. Good work Baz.

Baz helped nurses and doctors too. He would see them leave a room looking sad or worried about their patient and wag his tail at them. Their faces changed to a smile. A quick chat with Baz and they got on with their job, feeling a little bit better.

With every visit, Baz brings a bit of joy, a bit of hope, a bit of entertainment and a lot of comfort to people who are unwell. Me – well I'm the lucky person holding the lead, happy to watch the magic unfold.

And if Baz could talk, Cath thinks he would say: *'The secret to life is a big run in the park, followed by dinner and a good lie down. It doesn't get any better than that!'*

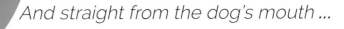

8

And straight from the dog's mouth ...

MOBY — TURNING FROWNS UPSIDE-DOWN

Hello! I'm Moby, a Bernese mountain dog, and I'm huge! There's a reason I'm so big and strong. My breed was bred for herding animals and protecting farms. But I have a different job. My job is fun, but super-important. I'm a therapy dog!

My job is to help kids who feel upset. I'm like a big plush toy that they can cuddle, pat and play with until they feel better. I'm going to show you a day in my job, so you'll see how important I am!

Each morning, I stand with a teacher at the school gates. As the children arrive, their faces light up. They fluff, ruffle, and pat my soft fur before heading to class. It's good that I'm big – I have lots

39

of fur to pat, so nobody misses out. Sometimes I think kids come to school just to see me! Seriously though, what's not to like? I'm happy, protective, brave and I do my job well.

I love digging and finding things. Sometimes I find a ball and the kids play with me. Sometimes, I pinch a ball and run, so the children chase me. I'm very fast, so I usually outrun them. That's what my strong legs are for. It takes several kids to corner me to retrieve their ball. Such fun! Occasionally I find something yucky to dig up. The kids take it from my mouth and put it in the bin.

After arrivals and games, I head to the office for a drink and a rest. Then it's time for more work. I wander about, visiting classrooms. I'm clumsy, and sometimes step on books or bump children with my tail. They don't mind – they laugh and pat me. Whew! So many pats!

Some classrooms have toys for me. I play with my drink bottle and sleep on the linoleum – it's nice and cold on hot days. Sometimes I sit on the mat with the class. When classroom visits are complete, I begin my serious job.

Off I go with the welfare team, visiting children around the school who need me. My job is to help them feel better. They may be feeling stressed, upset, anxious or angry. They can pat or play with me as they work on strategies with a welfare team member. I want every kid and teacher to be happy, and me doing my job well makes everyone happy.

When a kid is sad, I feel sad too. I nuzzle, cuddle and snuggle with them and let them know that it's okay to be upset and cry. Sometimes they think crying is babyish or wrong. I cuddle them and tell them crying is fine. We all cry sometimes. I cry too if I'm left alone too long, or I'm in trouble.

When a kid feels angry, they might think violence or saying mean things is okay. It's not okay and makes things worse. I tug on my leash and warn them. When they focus on me, they calm down and their anger fades. It's okay to be angry – it's not okay to take it out on others.

When a kid feels scared, I let them fluff my fur. I remind them things will soon be okay. When I feel scared, it feels never-ending too, but my number-one human cuddles me and tells me things will be alright. It works for me, so it can work for kids too!

I love every student in my school. They might think I'm just being a dog, but being a therapy dog is a tough job. I don't like seeing people sad. That's why I do the best job I can. I like seeing kids with positive attitudes!

I sometimes get to go for walks with teachers and children. I like walks! But walking me can be tricky. Sometimes I forget there's a teacher holding the lead, and when I dash off to chase something, that teacher comes flying with me! I don't mean any harm, of course. I just want to have fun.

I help everyone feel safe – my loud, strong barks will frighten off any danger, not to mention one look at my strong doggy muscles.

I understand that kids get sad or cranky. I get cranky and sad too! It's normal. When I get cranky, I bark loudly, but I never bark at the kids. I don't want them to be scared of me. I want to make kids happy! I want to make them smile! So, I keep my cool and stay a calm, happy dog.

After a busy day of turning frowns upside-down, I head home with my human. I have a game or two, eat my super-sized dinner and fall asleep.

And sleep peacefully knowing that when I wake up tomorrow, I get to start my day all over again!

KELSI — WITH HER CAME A HUGE SENSE OF RELIEF

The snoring coming from Alannah's bedroom can be heard at the other end of the house. I stop to look in on her on my way to bed. Kelsi the dog is asleep at Alannah's feet, snoring contentedly.

Alannah moves in her sleep, restless. Mid-snore, Kelsi is awake and checking, watching Alannah intently until she settles back to sleep. Kelsi gives me the look that says, 'all is fine, go to bed', tucks her head in and the snoring begins again.

I check the camera and monitor is on. Through it we can see Alannah from other rooms and hear Kelsi barking if help is needed.

I'm Caroline, Alannah's mum. Life has always been challenging for Alannah, but she's a fighter. Some of her challenges are epilepsy, communication problems and seizures, which happen suddenly, can be very frightening and cause her injury.

Alannah needs someone with her day and night. Once that was us, her family, with the help of a high-tech camera that monitored her. It meant we lived on high alert, constantly checking on Alannah. But two years ago, our whole world changed. Now her constant companion is Kelsi.

Before Kelsi, Alannah felt afraid to go out. She doesn't speak much, and her body doesn't always do what she needs it to do. But there was no choice. Although Alannah was frightened, she needed to attend many medical appointments and hospital trips.

When Alannah was eight, we researched seizure alert dogs. How wonderful it would be for Alannah to have a companion to help keep her safe and calm, alert us day and night if help were needed, and be a special friend at her side when things got tough. And so, the journey began.

After lots of paperwork, fundraising, visiting Smart Pups to meet the dogs, learning, and waiting, the exciting day came when we received the news that a Labrador cross golden retriever named Kelsi was a good match for Alannah. Kelsi then completed her training, learning skills and tasks specifically needed to help Alannah. When she finally arrived with her trainer, we spent a nervous week, learning the many commands we must know to give the best chance for Alannah and Kelsi. It couldn't have gone better.

Thirteen-year-old Alannah is happier, calmer and healthier with her loyal, devoted friend by her side and we, her family, are much more relaxed.

Kelsi is everything we had hoped for and more. She is smart, curious, attentive and loving, and she watches out for Alannah. She snuggles with Alannah to give comfort, disrupt meltdowns, picks up dropped items, pushes buttons, opens and closes doors and even takes off shoes, socks and jackets. Kelsi alerts an adult by barking when a seizure occurs, or Alannah needs help, day or night.

As a registered assistance dog, allowed to attend public places, Kelsi has opened a whole new world of possibilities and adventures for our family. She attends school with Alannah. It's a long trip but Kelsi snoozes in the car. School days are busy and full, and Kelsi is beside Alannah every moment. The children know not to approach Kelsi as she is working, but that doesn't stop Alannah and Kelsi entertaining the class with their antics and tricks.

Our family now goes on holidays, sometimes on planes, where Kelsi gets her own seat on the floor. We are free to go wherever we want to, shops, movies and restaurants. Kelsi even stays in hospital with Alannah when needed! Alannah is no longer afraid to go out.

Kelsi brought with her a huge sense of relief to our family. She is Alannah's best friend, who helps her with her daily challenges and doesn't judge what she can and can't do. She protects Alannah no matter what and gives her confidence to go to new places and try new things. Alannah often looks to make sure Kelsi is nearby.

Alannah struggles to communicate with humans, but not with her dog. She and Kelsi have their own way of communicating and that is special too.

Kelsi gets time off, as every dog must, and she loves soaking up the sun or snuggling into the comfort of her own 'off duty' crate. She loves games, including hide and seek. But mostly she loves being with Alannah. By helping Alannah, Kelsi has helped our whole family.

Sometimes Kelsi decides to seek out mischief but her 'I'm guilty' look gives her away. We pretend to be stern and firm, but Kelsi knows we are just big softies who are so incredibly grateful for all she does. Kelsi has won our hearts.

And if Kelsi could talk, Caroline thinks she would say: 'I love being with Alannah – busy days, school, adventures, hugs and a cosy bed. And I love pleasing the big people by letting them know when my girl needs help.'

BUDDY — THE START OF SOMETHING REALLY BIG

Buddy was a good dog with bad habits. He had been left to grow up alone in a paddock with nobody to play with or teach him manners. He was bored, unsociable and wild, and afraid of people and other dogs. He didn't know how to be any other way. He never had another dog to show him how to be polite so he would bare his teeth, growl and bark at them. He would be at the fence barking furiously whenever someone passed by.

I'm Cath. I was in the chainsaw shop in town one day when a woman approached me. She asked, 'Are those your ridgebacks outside in the ute?'

Thinking there was a problem I answered, 'Yes. Why?'

'Would you like another one?'

'Not really,' I replied. I didn't need another ridgeback — I already had three.

'He's six months old,' she continued. 'We don't have time for him anymore. We've moved to a new house and the yard is small and anyway, we don't want the hassle. His name's Buddy.'

I resisted asking why they got a dog in the first place if they didn't want the hassle.

'I'll discuss this with my partner. Give me your details.' Seriously, we'd already agreed three dogs was plenty. As far as I was concerned the conversation was over.

That night I began telling the story of the Rhodesian ridgeback in need of a home. I had barely begun when I heard, 'We'll have to take him.'

'What! Why?'

'Because he's obviously neglected and needs a good home.'

'Oh. Okay.'

Sometimes partners don't do what you expect.

I arranged to collect Buddy. It was raining heavily when I pulled up in front of a flash new house. A ridgeback stood shivering in the rain, imprisoned between the house wall, a fence and a steel gate.

No one answered the doorbell. Eventually I went around the side and approached the dog. He was soaking wet, trembling and miserable. I opened the gate and knelt. He didn't know what to do.

Was I a safe person or a threat? Not expecting this situation, I had left the lead in the ute.

'Come on boy,' I said, patting the side of my leg to encourage him. He followed me, and when I opened the tailgate, jumped straight in. We stared at each other. Then he leant forward and licked my chin.

'Okay, Buddy, you've got a new home.'

Things did not go smoothly. He chased the neighbours' chooks, bailed up strangers on the street and generally had a wild time. My other three dogs thought this interesting but too much work. They stayed chilled.

Buddy pulled on the lead, and wouldn't sit, stay or come when called. He loved exploring the bush, he loved running with the other dogs, and he loved me.

I put up a fence to save the community's chooks and keep passers-by from fear, and did lots of work with Buddy. Loose lead walking, coming when called, sitting and staying. With buckets of treats. A treat for looking at me. A treat for walking by my side. A treat for everything.

It worked. After three months Buddy had great manners. He loved hanging out with me.

I have a condition called bipolar II. This means there are times when I am incredibly sad and times when I am anxious. I have good medication and a great psychiatrist to help me. But when I was out and about — shopping, going into the city, at cafes, on public transport — I was always anxious. Not just a little nervous but throwing up in the gutter, panic attack anxious!

When Buddy was with me, I was much better. I would think about Buddy and not my fears. Buddy became my focus, not the people around me. I decided Buddy was going to be my assistance dog. If he could pass a Public Access Test, I could take him everywhere. But I couldn't find anyone to help me.

Finally, I found a trainer, who thought my idea was a great one. She agreed to run Buddy and me through a Public Access Test. We passed easily. After that Buddy came with me everywhere. With his vest and ID card we were a legal assistance-dog team.

But my psychiatrist wasn't happy. 'You are doing great, Cath, with Buddy. So now we need to help other people!'

So, I investigated the law, got a bunch of friends together, had a fundraising lunch and started an organisation called mindDog. That was 10 years ago. It took a huge amount of work by many people to get things up and running, but now we have more than 1400 assistance dogs helping people. And every year that number grows.

Buddy was the first mindDog and in my heart, the greatest ever. Buddy was the start of something really big.

And if Buddy could talk, Cath thinks he'd say:

'I do my best.'

HERMIONE — SCHOOL DOG INSIDE AND OUT

When Hermione began life as a school dog, pretty much all she did was distract students from their work! It wasn't Hermione's fault. It's just that she looked so cute and cuddly that students wanted to pet her all the time!

Hermione was a six-month-old puppy, so it was a bit overwhelming to meet 700 students. But she quickly settled in and made the school, the staff and students her own.

It was our principal's idea to get a school dog. Dogs can provide a lot of pleasure and comfort for the children – and adults too. I'm Loris, a teacher librarian, and it was decided that Hermione, my Cavalier King Charles spaniel puppy, could try out for the job. It all worked out beautifully and now Hermione comes to school with me each day.

Based in the library, Hermione greets visitors and students doing their reading and research. She has a bed, some cushions and several favourite high spots to watch from, and she joins in activities if she wishes. Sometimes she falls asleep and everyone chuckles when her loud snores break the silence of our reading lessons! Students are used to her now, so she still gets pats and cuddles, but everyone gets on with their school tasks. Hermione is loved by all, but to our surprise her biggest fans are the senior boys. They make a fuss of her and carry her about like a baby.

Another surprise is how many extra daily guests the library has now. There were people who rarely came in, yet now they are daily visitors. Hermione is the first to be greeted, after which people remember to talk to the library humans!

Hermione helps anxious children to relax. She helps new students settle in. She even helps children to make new friends as they meet in the library to visit Hermione or take her for a walk or to play. She gives shy kids something to talk about and share. So many new friendships have been made over the soft, fluffy coat of Hermione.

One new girl was terrified of dogs, and her family was concerned there was a school dog. When the girl met Hermione for the first time she felt afraid, but Hermione's calm, sweet and gentle nature worked a treat, and soon the girl was happily patting her. The next day she returned to visit again, and before long she brought in her mother and sister to meet Hermione. They were amazed. Now the girl visits the library every morning to greet Hermione.

Hermione has a group of fans who come to cuddle and groom her regularly. She adores them and makes a beeline for her friends every day! Other students are dedicated dog walkers, while others teach her obedience tasks and tricks.

It's a two-way street, people look after Hermione and she looks after them. She is a perfect listener for those who don't want to share their problem with a human. Around Hermione people seem to relax, slow down and enjoy a quiet moment – preferably while giving her tummy rubs!

Sometimes Hermione leaves the library for special jobs. If a student is upset, the counsellor may ask to borrow her for a bit. Hermione cheerfully heads off to be cuddled by a child needing comfort. Sometimes an upset child may want to go home, but after half an hour of cuddling Hermione they are calm enough to return to class. Sometimes having tears licked from your hands by a sympathetic dog can make all the difference, and it's very hard to stay angry when you are cuddling a dog.

Hermione knows when people feel sad and responds by sitting quietly close by. Even if a sad child doesn't know she is there, she stays put and ignores all other offers until she is satisfied the child is okay again.

Hermione is a model for art class. Walking her is an activity for a child unable to participate in sport. She features in school newsletters, and on goes the list of duties she has.

The highlight of Hermione's day is being outside at lunchtime. What fun, freedom and excitement to wander freely amongst students, hoovering up dropped food scraps and chasing birds! An after-lunch snooze is a must after all that exertion!

Now aged two, Hermione's personality has emerged from playful pup to determined and wilful 'teenager'. Everyone at our school loves her gentle presence and the joy she brings each day. She's been voted the most indulged dog in the world by our school community!

And if Hermione could speak, Loris thinks she would say:

'I love Loris, going to school, big kids, little kids, the library, cuddles, making people feel better, puppacinos, bird chasing, walks, everything about my life, but best of all I love OUTSIDE!'

MAX — LIVING LIFE TO THE MAX IS WHAT WE DO

Max and I love superheroes. He has his own Superman cape, and we get about in a cool van painted with superheroes. Max is a bit of a star himself. He's appeared in television advertisements and on a show about dogs, and he's well known in our local community.

I'm James. I'm 21 years old and I live on a small farm with my parents and my dog, Max. I have cerebral palsy. That means my brain doesn't always send the right messages to my body, so it makes moving the way I want to move difficult. Even things like drinking from a cup or using a knife and fork can be tricky. I can't walk so I use a wheelchair to get around.

Life is busy though. I go to college two days a week. My van is designed to carry me in my wheelchair and Max. I can't drive, so my carer drives us to college. Max stays beside me while I study. I go to the gym twice a week and Max watches while I work out. I enjoy music, play guitar and attend a music program. Max loves music class. I think he likes music as much as I do.

I met Max a year ago. He's my mobility dog and best friend. I'd been on a waiting list so when we received a call from the Mobility Assistance Dogs Trust, telling us there was a dog that was a match for me, I was very excited. Mum and I travelled to meet Max and stayed at the training facility for two weeks. We got to know Max, learned how to look after him and keep up his training so he could help me when I needed a hand. Max had completed two years of training and was qualified.

Max helps me to be independent. It's frustrating needing to rely on people. Now, with Max, I am never alone, and I feel safer and more confident.

Max does tasks I find hard to do. He opens doors, drawers, and cupboards, puts my washing in the basket, fetches and hands me things, pushes the pedestrian crossing button, turns on lights, takes off my socks, and brings his food bowl at dinner time. Each night he carries his sleeping mat to the bedroom and puts the van keys on the side table ready for the morning.

Max and I have our share of fun and adventures. Appearing in adverts and TV shows involved flying to the city for filming and being followed around by film crews, getting our hair done so we looked the part, and lots of hours of filming. Max behaved like a superstar and didn't miss a beat.

With Max's help, I would like to help children learn. We visited a school last year and the children really loved Max. He wore his Superman cape, and I wore my Superman T-shirt. Max demonstrated to the children the tasks he can do, and they learned about mobility dogs. The children also read books to him. Next year we want to visit

more schools so that Max can teach more children and help them with reading.

Life has really changed since Max came. He comes everywhere with me. I meet a lot of new people now, as people like to talk about Max. Max wears a jacket that lets people know he is working and mustn't be distracted. It's tricky though, as Max loves people and people love Max, so sometimes I must work hard to keep him focused on his job.

Max loves water. Sometimes he jumps in the lake or river for a swim. Now that's okay, except Max needs to be clean and well-groomed when he goes out in public. One day we were ready to leave when we noticed Max had snuck off. We found him in the middle of a puddle, black and muddy from his tummy down. This made us late, which caused a bit of drama. Naughty Max!

At home Max sits with me while I play computer games and listen to music. He loves walks, and our family walk around the farm together. Max finds places to sniff out interesting smells, runs, plays, and tries to sneak in a dip in the river.

Max and I love life, having adventures, hanging out and achieving stuff. You could say we live life to the max. Max has not just changed my life; things are easier for my parents and they love him too. I am so grateful to everyone who raised and trained Max and feel incredibly lucky to have him as my friend and helper. Max is my superhero.

And if Max could talk, James thinks he would say: *'It's great being a mobility dog. I can go everywhere with my best friend James, even to the movies, and I love helping him do what he wants to do.'*

And straight from the dog's mouth ...

ALICE — LEAVING PAWPRINTS OF LOVE

'm Alice, a Cavalier King Charles spaniel. When I was four, I came to live with Bob and Lynne. My first family had moved overseas, and I was staying with a family who had a fast and bouncy dog. It wasn't working well. I prefer the slower side of life. One night I went for a sleepover with Bob and Lynne, and never looked back. The three of us were a perfect fit!

Straight away I could see how much I was needed. Bob had an illness called dementia. That meant he had trouble remembering things, and he was often confused. Being forgetful and confused can be scary, and if Bob wandered off, he could easily get lost.

Bob had another illness too, which made him wobbly and jerky. But still, he could walk, so the three of us enjoyed walking slowly together. Bob liked looking at the ocean, followed by cake at an outdoor cafe.

When I was with Bob, he was calmer and happier. I decided my purpose in life was to be a dementia assistance dog. I began keeping Bob company and making sure he was safe. That helped Lynne a lot. She taught me sign language, so I could follow her instructions without waking or confusing Bob. So long as Bob could see me, he didn't wander off, feel afraid, sad or upset. I stayed beside him every moment I could.

As time went on, Bob forgot more things. He became more confused. He found it harder to do everyday things and needed a wheelchair. Being a smart and caring dog, I adapted my routine to make sure Bob stayed safe. I decided to sleep at the top of the stairs, so that if Bob left the bedroom my loud barking could alert Lynne. I would walk in front of Bob, so that he knew I was there. I snuggled in to comfort him. I made sure he stayed safe. If I was concerned, I barked until Lynne came.

A day came when Bob needed care in hospital. I was allowed a daily visit and we would spend time cuddling and snoozing together. Even in hospital, Bob was calmer and happier when I was there.

But Bob didn't come home. I felt miserable. I lay about and showed no interest in doing anything. Lynne worried about me. One day she saw an advertisement for Story Dogs and decided that a new job might be just what we both needed. We applied, learned some new skills and I passed my exam first time!

My new job is to help children to read. What an awesome job to have! There are some children who don't want to read. Others are easily distracted. Some lack confidence and are shy to read aloud to people. But all the children want to read to me.

So once a week, after a bath, off we go to school. I'm dressed in my official coat and sometimes wear a hat!

We have our own space. So, I sit and wait, but never for long. One by one, children come to read me wonderful stories and show me pictures. I snuggle in and pay attention as children relax and gain confidence and skill. Children who wouldn't read before, now wait patiently for their timeslot to read to me. I show them that reading can be fun and I get lots of cuddles. It's magic! And sometimes I'm invited to do special jobs, like listen to reading at the local library.

But wait, there's more! Now I have another job as well. I never run out of cuddles to give, so Lynne and I visit people in an aged care facility. There people love to cuddle and talk to a dog, so I spread my love around. People in wheelchairs, young or old, are a special attraction. Perhaps they remind me of Bob. I've heard it said that my big brown eyes and distinguished eyebrows melt people's hearts.

And hey, in between my two jobs I have fun too. I'm not much into walking as I have some arthritis in my ankle, but I really love biking. I ride in the basket behind Lynne and we head off for adventures, picnics, the beach, and outdoor concerts. I really love food, so I am a little chubby. Lynne does her best to keep me slim, but I'm sneaky and it's hard to stop me from eating any food I can find!

I'm a dog who is full of love. From dementia dog to a dog who listens to stories and goes visiting, that's me. I love everyone – children, the elderly and everyone in between – and nothing pleases me more than to make them feel happy, safe and loved.

I'm Awesome Alice, leaving paw prints of love wherever I go.

14

EBONY — MY PILLS ON FOUR LEGS

I'm Donna. For 20 years I was in the Navy. My job was repairing and maintaining helicopters. That job ended when I had a nasty accident. After that, I was always in pain from my injuries. I began having nightmares, flashbacks, anxiety and depression. Depression is when someone feels incredibly sad and can't make that feeling go away, even when life is good. There's a nickname for that, depression is known as the black dog. This story is about a real black dog who saved me.

After my job ended, I stayed home for 10 years. I avoided crowds and noises. I was often in hospital. I needed to take so many pills each day that I could not think clearly. Sadly, that meant my family had to go out and enjoy life without me.

Elsewhere, a black Labrador puppy began learning to be a guide dog for a blind person. She was smart, obedient, gentle and learned her lessons quickly. But she was very playful, and when she spied another dog, she'd dash off to play with them. Now that wouldn't work for a blind person, as they wouldn't see other dogs coming, so it was decided this pup might be suited to a different job, helping someone who could see.

Another organisation, Integra Service Dogs, took over her training. She was named Ebony and she learned her new job well, to help a veteran who was struggling with life.

I was overjoyed when I received the call to say that I was to be given Ebony. That was three years ago, and everything changed after that.

When Ebony first arrived, we stayed home together and got to know each other. Then one day we cautiously went out, with Ebony on her lead. She was very well mannered. With the help of a wonderful trainer, we learned to do things and go places together.

Slowly, I became part of the world again, with Ebony beside me. When I have flashbacks, she distracts me by scratching my knee with her paw. When I am anxious, she nudges my leg, to let me know she's right there. When I'm sad, she cuddles me. When I have nightmares, she wakes me by pushing me with her paws. In crowds she stands behind or in front of me so people can't come close. That helps me a lot!

Thanks to Ebony I have my life back. I play golf, eat out or see a movie with Ebony at my side. I enjoy life with my family instead of staying home alone. We've even been on trips by plane and boat! We love hitting the road on our motorbike, behind which we tow Ebony's purpose-built trailer. Her trailer has a bed, air conditioner, light, and a hatch to stick her head out and get the wind in her hair. When the bike is started, Ebony grabs her very own motorcycle jacket and runs to her trailer. No way she's being left behind! Off we go, touring the country on our bike. And to think before Ebony I couldn't get past my own front door!

Now I do public speaking and fundraising – can you believe that? Ebony caused much laughter when she once sat next to me at a speech and howled. Everyone thought she was making her own speech!

Ebony is playful, adventurous and makes us laugh. She danced like a champ at a party one night and another time approached Santa and sat for a photo shoot. At home she steals our socks, so that we chase her. She tries to help solve our problems. When our car was bogged on a beach, we dug sand from around the wheels, and she dug it all back again!

Ebony loves playgrounds and going down the slide! She plays ball, still loves other dogs, and runs with her pals at the park. Tired out, she happily snoozes with Mushy, her plush dog toy.

I will always have thoughts and feelings that challenge me, but with Ebony I can accept this – and move on. I've gone from taking twelve pills daily to only three. Ebony has become my 'pills on four legs'.

Each day Ebony needs a walk, so I must leave the house. I feel safe with her, she is a blessing in my life. It's a win-win. I do for her and she does for me. I plan to play more golf, tour the countryside, and make up for lost time with my family. I also raise awareness of assistance dog etiquette, because not everyone understands that dogs in jackets should not be distracted.

My black dog, Ebony was the key to taming the black dog!

And if Ebony could talk, Donna thinks she would say:
'If I am sleeping on you and you cannot move you must sleep in – it is the law! For I am your "pills on four legs" and I know best.'

GIDGET — FURRY EARS THAT MAKE A WORLD OF DIFFERENCE

Gidget is a very special dog. She hears sounds for me at home that I cannot hear, as I am nearly deaf. Not only is Gidget a qualified hearing assistance dog, she is also my best friend!

I'm Elizabeth, and Gidget can go wherever I go. We go all over the place together, visiting people, doing so many things and sharing many adventures together. She can even fly sitting next to me on a plane if I travel, and she always gets the window seat, although she must stay on the floor.

When Gidget comes out with me she must wear her uniform. That uniform is an orange jacket with 'Australian Lions Hearing Dogs' on it and an orange collar and leash. I must also wear a lanyard with her name, photo and number, as well as carry her official card, which says that she is a service dog.

Gidget is trained to respond to nine sounds. They are the doorbell or door knock, the landline phone, mobile phone, alarm clock, oven, microwave, whistling kettle, a baby crying and the smoke detector. She also knows how to go and fetch someone if I need help.

When Gidget hears a sound, she will find me and jump up with two paws. She is saying 'There's a sound, follow me.' When we reach the sound, I give her a treat to say, 'Job well done.'

The exception is the smoke detector. Gidget knows this is an extremely important, lifesaving sound and if she hears it she immediately finds me, touches me with two paws and drops down onto her tummy, staring at me until I respond.

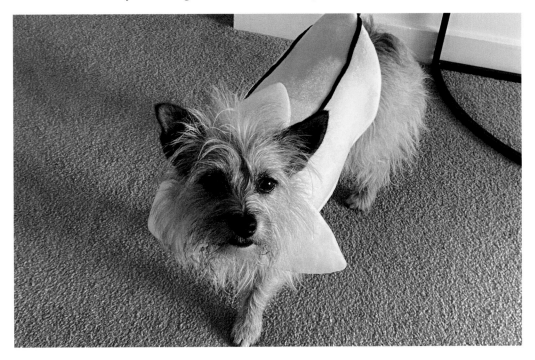

Gidget is not allowed on the furniture, as she is not a pet dog. The only time she is allowed on the furniture is to alert me to a sound.

Gidget wakes me up every morning when my alarm goes off. It's a wonderful way to start the day with my best friend jumping on me saying, 'Time to get up, lazy!' So, up I get, in a great mood for the day.

I never miss a phone call anymore, as Gidget always tells me the phone is ringing and the call is streamed through my smart hearing aids via bluetooth. I don't burn anything in the kitchen either, as Gidget lets me know when the oven or microwave timers go off. That's a safer and much more fun way to cook, that's for sure!

Many hearing dogs are dogs who have been unwanted or abandoned, so they come in all shapes and sizes, keen to have a new start in life. Gidget is a golden, scruffy looking terrier cross. She will soon be six years old, so she has many years left as a hearing dog, before her time comes for retirement.

Gidget loves her toys and enjoys tearing them to pieces! She loves the liver treats that I give her for sound work and raw bones, which she chomps up really fast! She also enjoys going to the park, where she can be just like other dogs. There she sees her many friends, who are dogs and people! She also likes to play catch, where she jumps high to catch a ball and bring it back to me.

Gidget and I live in a high-rise building, so we have no backyard. That means that to take Gidget to the toilet, we go to the nearby park several times a day. Where I live, everybody knows the two of us. We are out and about every day and up to something new and exciting. After an active day's work answering sounds and going with me wherever I go, Gidget looks forward to her special high-energy dinner. Dinner time is the best time of the day for Gidget.

Gidget is my 'furry ears' which I couldn't manage without. I love Gidget very much. She has given me so much. I never go anywhere without her and never would. We share a very special bond, different to that with a pet dog. That's because Gidget does so much for me to makes my life easier, safer and much more fun!

If Gidget could talk, Elizabeth thinks she would say: 'I love you very much and I know you love to get dressed up to go out, so I get dressed up too! I have such a fun life, going everywhere that you do!'

And a twist in the tale ... sometimes dogs have disabilities too

HUNTER — SOMETIMES WE NEED TO THINK A BIT DIFFERENTLY

We welcomed our pup Hunter into our home as a ball of white fluff. He was gentle, loving, and great company for my wife, Kate, who has been unable to work since she had heart surgery at 23. Kate is home a lot, and a dog makes a perfect companion.

I'm Charlie. Kate and I have had dogs before and trained them to be obedient and well mannered. So as Hunter grew from fluff ball to bouncy youngster, we began teaching him basic commands. We got nowhere! We knew Hunter was smart, as he proved this daily in many ways, but he never responded to commands.

When he turned four months old, we decided we needed advice. We contacted a trainer. We followed every instruction and suggestion for obedience lessons and practised daily. Still nothing worked. Hunter never came when called or followed the simplest command!

Something wasn't right. One night, while Hunter was snoozing in his bed, I had an idea. I fetched a metal pot and spoon from the kitchen. Standing close to Hunter I began banging the pot. A booming, metallic noise filled the room. Hunter didn't budge. He didn't even raise an eyebrow. He slept on. That's when we knew he was deaf. Next day, the vet confirmed Hunter had no hearing at all and was most likely born that way.

We were determined to give Hunter the best life possible, but nervous about how we could teach him obedience, keep him safe and help him understand we loved him, without him being able to hear our voices. We did a lot of research to try and find useful information but found no-one with a puppy that was born deaf.

Well, when a person cannot hear, sometimes they choose to communicate with sign language. We decided to try to teach Hunter our own version of sign language. It was trial and error, but we owed it to Hunter to give it our best shot.

We began with simple hand and finger signs so as not to confuse him. First, we tried to teach Hunter to sit on command. We had to make sure he was looking at us before we began. Our sign was index finger down. When Hunter watched and decided to sit down, we made a fuss and rewarded him. He caught on quickly, and soon he would sit when he saw the sign and enjoy the fuss and treat. We were on the right track.

When it was time for a walk, we made a walking motion with our two middle fingers, and Hunter would run to his lead. For mealtime we made circles with our index finger, as he runs around in circles, excited about dinner. When we want Hunter to know he's done well, we shake our thumb and give him the thumbs up. Gradually we added more commands. Hunter now knows many and is a happy and obedient dog.

Hunter brings incredible love and joy to Kate as her companion and friend. They spend every day together and learn from each other. Hunter uses his facial expressions and paws to tell us what he wants, and Kates teaches him new hand signals. He loves learning. It's a work in progress as he is still only three.

It can be difficult to comprehend the impact of deafness on a dog. Social things puppies learn, like hearing and responding to other dogs' barks or growls, cannot happen. A dog relies on their ears way more than humans do and can hear sounds that humans cannot hear. It's rare for a dog to be born completely deaf.

Hunter loves water, and swims in the pool in summer. In winter he is a cuddly dog, who wants to sit on our laps, although at 40 kilograms that can be tricky.

He loves people and meeting other dogs. His best mate is Bruno, who sometimes comes to stay. Bruno alerts Hunter to visitors and noises by his movements, and helps Hunter be aware of things around him.

When out walking, Hunter must stay on this lead, as he won't know to come back if he isn't looking at me, nor hear dangerous situations. But at our park there are times when I chase him as he tries to play hide and seek!

We feel incredibly lucky to have a beautiful dog that is loving, caring, sensitive and deaf. Like everyone with a disability, human or animal, sometimes we need to think a bit differently, try a little harder, and take a little longer to find a way to overcome. The rewards are life-changing for everyone.

For us, having Hunter in our family feels as though it was meant to be.

And if Hunter could talk, Charlie thinks he would say:

'I'm not missing a thing. Life is perfect and I can't imagine it any other way.'

ABOUT THE AUTHOR

Author Gina Dawson is a former teacher and counsellor, who presented programs on a variety of social issues in schools for fifteen years. She is a lifelong lover of dogs, an experienced trainer, and is cognisant of the disability sector, with a particular interest in mental health.

Gina's passion is writing books for children and young people that promote awareness about personal and social issues. *With a Dog's Love* was written to raise awareness of the important roles that dogs with jobs play, helping individuals and society in a variety of ways.

In addition to children's books, Gina also ghost-writes memoirs for adults, as well as the occasional short story. She is a volunteer for an assistance dog organisation. In her spare time, Gina enjoys, in no particular order, dog training, reading, walking, architecture, travelling, spending time with family and friends and, of course the company of her dog and great mate, Kiera, an Australian Kelpie.

With a Dog's Love is her ninth book.